WHY SEALS BLOW THEIR NOSES

WHY SEALS BLOW THEIR NOSES

Canadian Wildlife in Fact & Fiction

Diane Swanson

Illustrations by Douglas Penhale

WHITECAP BOOKS • VANCOUVER • TORONTO

Copyright © 1992 by Diane Swanson
Whitecap Books
Vancouver/Toronto

Edited by Bruce Obee
Cover design by Warren Clark
Interior design by Carolyn Deby
Cover illustration and interior illustrations by Douglas Penhale

Typeset by CompuType, Vancouver, B.C.

Printed and bound in Canada by D.W. Friesen and Sons Ltd., Altona, Manitoba

Canadian Cataloguing in Publication Data

Swanson, Diane, 1944-
  Why seals blow their noses

  Includes index.
  ISBN 1-55110-038-X

  1. Zoology—North America—Juvenile literature.
  2. Animals—Juvenile literature.   I. Title.
  QL49.S93   1992   j591   C92-091529-9

The publisher acknowledges the assistance of the Canada Council and the Cultural Services Branch of the government of British Columbia in making this publication possible.

Acknowledgements

Sincere thanks to the following for reviewing sections of this book: Dave Fraser of Arenaria Research and Interpretation, Robin Baird of Simon Fraser University and the Marine Mammal Research Group, Ralph Archibald of the B.C. Ministry of Forests, Nancy Sherwood of the University of Victoria, David Nagorsen of the Royal British Columbia Museum, Barry Saunders of the B.C. Ministry of Environment, Lands and Parks, and private consultant Wayne Swanson.

And special thanks to storyteller Penny Draper for suggestions and advice, and to editor Bruce Obee and publisher Colleen MacMillan for guidance and encouragement.

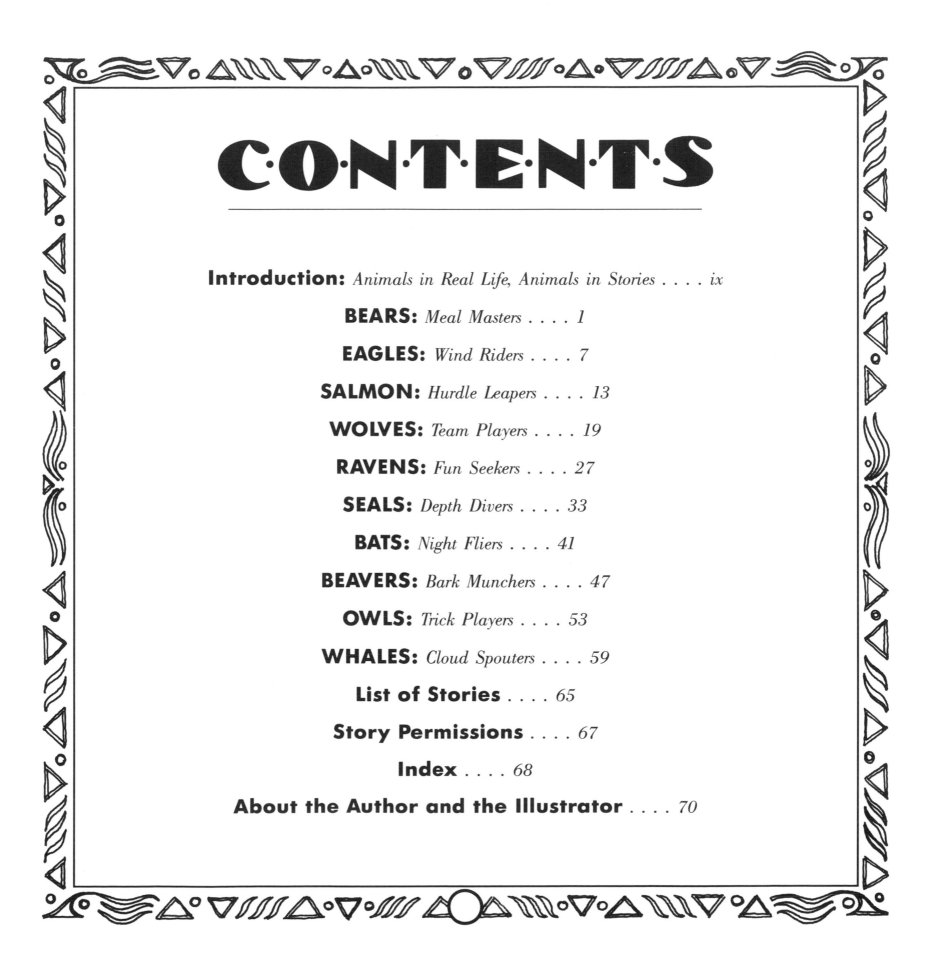

C·O·N·T·E·N·T·S

INTRODUCTION

Animals in Real Life, Animals in Stories

Animals are amazing—even amusing—and Canada's animals are no exception. Hooded seals blow big, red "balloons" out of their nostrils. Ravens toboggan down snowbanks, head first. Wolves "talk" to each other, using sounds and body language. And bears snorkel through rivers to catch salmon.

Not surprisingly, people around the world love to tell animal stories. They've been passing them on for centuries—first by word of mouth, then by writing them down. One old story from Japan tells of a whale meeting Buddha. Another, from Africa, tells how bats became night creatures. And one story—told in various ways in Norway, Sweden and Canada—explains why bears have short tails.

Animals in stories live on and on. But in real life, there are fewer animals now than there once were. As more people spread across Canada, they hunted many animals. And they left fewer natural places for animals to live.

Today, more people treasure animals. Many Canadians want to make sure that animals always have a place in Canada—in real life as well as in stories.

B·E·A·R·S

Meal Masters

Lots of bears live on bookshelves: Winnie the Pooh, Yogi Bear, Baloo—the jungle bear—and more. Bears in stories are great, but in real life, bears are even better. They're handsome creatures, curious about their world and everything in it. And lots of them live in Canada.

Canada and the Three Bears

Many countries in the northern half of the world have bears; Canada has three different kinds: black bears, grizzly bears and polar bears. They're all big and furry with short legs and stubby tails.

The black bear is the smallest of the three, but it weighs up to 270 kilograms. An average man weighs about 75 kilograms. Black bears live in forests right across Canada. It's true that many of them are black, but others are brown, bluish, cinnamon or white.

Why Bears Have Short Tails

One winter, a fox said to a bear: "Stick your long tail through a hole in the ice on the river. If you sit very still, fish will bite your tail. Then pull it out suddenly and you will pull the fish out with it. The longer you stay, the more fish you'll catch."

The bear did just as the fox said. But no fish bit the bear's tail. What's worse, the water froze hard all around it. When the bear pulled very hard, its long tail snapped right off, leaving just a stump. And that's why bears have very short tails.

—a story from Norway, Sweden, eastern Canada and the Nakotcho-Kutchin of northern Canada

Grizzly bears weigh more than twice as much as black bears. Grizzlies live in the forests and mountains of western Canada. Their long, thick fur ranges from dark brown to pale yellow, and it is usually grizzled—streaked with grey. These bears are also known for their humped backs.

The biggest bears in Canada are polar bears. One can weigh 700 kilograms. Polar bears live on ice and snow throughout the Arctic. The hairs of their coats are as clear as glass, but they reflect so much light they make the bears look white or pale yellow.

When Bears Get Hungry

Black bears and grizzlies feed mostly on plants, but they also eat some meat and fish. Polar bears, on the other hand, feed mostly on meat and fish, but they also eat a few plants.

Bears Harvest

All three kinds of bears gobble berries and graze wild grasses. Sometimes, polar bears also munch on seaweed. Black bears and grizzlies nibble the new growth on twigs. They use their long, sharp claws to dig up roots and to slash beehives for honey—a favourite food, but one they don't often find.

Bears Hunt

Black bears and grizzlies hunt big animals, like deer, elk and moose as well as little animals, like ants, grasshoppers and mice. Polar bears mainly hunt seals, walruses and young whales.

Some people think that strength makes the bear a good hunter. After all, one whack from a grizzly's paw can break the back of an elk. But a bear's keen senses are just as useful. A polar bear can smell a seal beneath ice and snow a metre thick. Bears can hear small animals scurry underground. And although their eyes seem small, bears see at least as well as people do. Even under water, polar bears can spot shellfish on a shallow seafloor.

Speed also makes bears good hunters. Their heavy fur coats and layers of fat make them look slow-moving—but don't believe it. Grizzlies can run, twisting and turning, up to 60 kilometres per hour for short distances. That's fast enough to catch a horse. Even on ice, polar bears can

Why Bears Also Eat Meat

A farmer and a bear decided to sow a crop and share what they grew. The first year, they planted wheat and the farmer told the bear: "I'll take the top half. You can have the bottom."

But at harvest time, the bear was very unhappy. All the grain went to the farmer, and the bear got only the stems.

The next spring, the bear told the farmer: "I will take the top half this time."

The farmer changed the crop to turnips. At harvest time, the bottom half—the vegetable, which grows underground—went to the farmer. The bear got only the stems and leaves. Angrily, it stomped off into the woods, and after that, bears hunted animals and ate meat as well as plants.

—*a story from Holland and eastern Europe*

run up to 40 kilometres per hour. The hair on the bottoms of their feet keeps them from slipping.

Bears Fish

Grizzlies and black bears are especially good at fishing. They may use their jaws to snap leaping salmon right out of the air or grab one from the water. Or they may stand still until a fish swims by, then—in the flash of a paw—pin it down or knock it out of the stream. Sometimes a bear will go "snorkelling"— wading with all but its ears underwater—until its powerful jaws can grab a fish.

When Bears Reproduce

Bears mate in early summer, but bear cubs do not start to form inside their mother until about December. By that time, she is sleeping in a cave or den—something she does most of the winter. If she is fit and fat enough to live until spring without eating, the bear cubs start to develop inside her.

The largest newborn bear cub, a polar bear, weighs only as much as a small bag of sugar. Its mother is about 350 times heavier. Human mothers weigh about 20 times more than their new babies.

The bear cub is not well developed at birth. It has a hairless, pinkish-white body. Its eyes— shut tight—see nothing for 30 to 40 days. Its legs are poorly formed and it can barely move.

New cubs get little help from their mother. Because she is sleeping the winter away, she is not very aware of them. The cubs snuggle up to their mother's furry body to keep warm and get milk.

Occasionally, the mother wakes up. She may lick her cubs, rub them with her nose or draw them closer. Then she falls back to sleep. But her real job doesn't begin until spring when the cubs are ready to learn how to live like bears.

When Bears Meet People

As big and strong as bears are, they rarely attack people. In fact, when bears sense someone coming, they usually head the other way. If people get too close, some bears try to scare them away by making loud noises. Others may charge at full speed, then stop suddenly.

When bears attack, they are not being mean. A very hungry polar bear may attack a person for food. But most bears attack people to defend themselves or their cubs. A mother bear will do almost anything to protect her young. If she has to, she will even fight to the death to save them.

Still, very few people die from bear attacks. When you think how much bigger and stronger bears are, that's really amazing.

△　　△　　△

Canada does not have as many bears as it once did. In some places, people killed too many bears for meat, fur or body parts, like claws. In others, people changed the land so much that bears can't live there any more. But today, many people are working to make sure that Canada will always have room for its three bears.

How People Became Wary of Bears

A woman came across a house where bearskins lay in the entrance. She went in and found that the people of the house were really bears in human form. She stayed with them for a while and often watched a big bear put on its skin to go hunting for food.

When the woman decided to return to her people, the big bear warned her: "Don't tell people about us. They might come and kill my cubs."

One day, the woman could keep her secret no longer. She told her husband what she had seen. At once, the people took off after the bears, and the big bear came after the woman. Dogs surrounded the bear and attacked it, but the bear struck back.

Suddenly, all of them grew bright. They rose up to the sky and became stars—stars that form the shape of barking dogs around a bear. After that, people were wary of bears.

—*a story from the Inuit of the Arctic*

E·A·G·L·E·S

Wind Riders

If people call you an "eagle eye," it means you notice everything around you. If they say you "soar with the eagles," it means you are doing very well. Language—and stories—connect eagles with lots of good things. That's because many people respect them so much.

Eagles are strong and handsome. They are skilled, graceful fliers. And they have eyes so keen they can see you when you can't see them—not even as specks in the sky.

Eagles are one of biggest birds on Earth. With wings outstretched, some kinds span more than two metres—more than the length of your bed. And they live on every continent, except Antarctica.

In Canada, there are two kinds: the bald eagle, which lives near seashores, rivers and lakes; and the golden eagle, which lives in hilly country and

The Eagle Must Fly

One evening, a hunter caught a live golden eagle and took it to the palace of Osman the Great. Osman was very pleased. But his favourite slave, Mohamet, begged him to let the bird go. "The eagle must be free to soar through the sky," said Mohamet.

Still, Osman told his other slaves: "Chain the eagle's foot to a heavy metal ball so it can't fly, but care for it well."

Each day, the slaves served the eagle fresh meat and water in silver bowls. But the bird only wanted to fly.

Finally, Mohamet could stand it no longer. Sneaking past the other slaves, he took the metal ball off the chain. "You can have what I cannot—your freedom," he said to the eagle. "Now, fly away with the chain. It will remind you that you were once a slave like me."

—*a story from Germany*

mountains. Both are dark brown, but the bald eagle has a white head, neck and tail. It was named for its white colouring (an old meaning for bald is "white"). The golden eagle was named for the gold feathers on its head and neck.

In the Sky

In flight, eagles are quite a sight. They can speed across the sky faster than cars along a highway. With a few beats of their long, powerful wings, they rise higher. Then, they dive towards the ground.

To save energy, eagles ride the wind. They glide across the sky with air currents. Sometimes, they make their wings stiff and catch an upcurrent, spiralling higher and higher in the air.

The eagle is built to fly. Besides its huge wings, its body is smooth and shaped to slide easily through the air. And to make itself even smoother, the eagle flies with its head straight out and its legs tucked in.

The eagle is also a very nimble flier. It can twist and turn in flight—even flip onto its back. It can fly high, swoop part-way down, then do a somersault in midair.

Sometimes a pair of bald eagles will lock claws with each other before somersaulting. Together, they fall for hundreds of metres before letting go and soaring up again. Scientists think this might be a way of courting a mate—or fighting.

On the Hunt

Eagles eat the flesh of animals, like fish, rabbits, snakes, birds, young deer—even foxes. When they catch lots of food, they eat lots. That's so they can live a few days without eating when food is hard to find.

The eagle is well-equipped to hunt:
- Its large eyes see very far ahead as well as to the sides.

Eagles often hunt alone, but sometimes they work together. One may distract an animal while the other attacks it from behind. Or one eagle may swoop down on an animal, making it run towards the other eagle.

Sometimes, eagles hunt like pirates. They snatch fish away from other birds or scare them into dropping their catch.

Special see-through eyelids protect the eyes from dust and bright sunshine.

- Its strong, hooked beak is great for tearing food into pieces.
  A wading bald eagle may also use its beak to grab salmon that are laying and fertilizing eggs in streams.
- Its big, strong feet and sharp, curved claws snatch and kill animals. Because the bald eagle eats lots of slippery fish, the soles of its feet are covered with rough scales. They improve the eagle's grip.

Why Eagles See Well

An eagle was asked to fly to the top of a tall tree so it could watch for war canoes. That way it could warn the village of danger. But the eagle couldn't see well—not like the snail.

So the eagle told the snail: "You must trade eyes with me so I can help the village."

"Alright," agreed the snail. "But you must bring my eyes back."

The eagle flew to the tree and looked out—far, far across the water. Soon he spotted a war canoe and warned the chief at once.

When the trouble had passed, the eagle flew down from the tree, and the snail demanded its eyes back. But the eagle decided to keep them forever. And that's why snails move so slowly today, and eagles see so well.

—a story from the Kwakwaka'wakw (formerly called the Kwakiutl) of Canada

The Eagle and the Snake

High in the sky, an eagle spotted a snake. The mighty bird swooped down and grabbed it. But at once, the snake threw its coils around the bird. The two fought for their lives.

Just then, a man came along and helped the eagle fight off the snake. The lucky bird flew off, and that made the snake very an-gry. When the man wasn't looking, the snake spat poison into his drinking water.

Feeling hot after the fight, the man decid-ed to have a drink. But the eagle had been watching from above. Just in time, it swooped down and knocked the water from the man's hand, saving his life.

—*a story from Greece (one of Aesop's fables)*

In the Nest

Eagles usually mate for life. As a pair, they build a nest high in treetops or on cliff ledges where they can watch out for danger. They make their nest out of twigs and branches. But they line it with softer things, like moss, grass, pine needles or seaweed. If people live close by, eagles may even work bits of clotheslines into their nests.

Eagles use a nest over and over, making it bigger each year. One famous nest in the United States was 36 years old when a hurricane blew it down. It was more than three metres tall and weighed about 1800 kilograms—approximately the weight of a station wagon.

A female eagle usually lays two eggs in the nest. She keeps them warm—with some help from her mate—but she gets especially busy when the eggs hatch.

Young eaglets are helpless. Their thin covering exposes them to hot sun and cold nights. Their light colour attracts enemies, like owls. So the mother eagle tries to keep the eaglets com-fortable and safe beneath her wing.

At first, the father eagle hunts food for them all. When he brings it to the nest, the mother tears it into tiny strips for the eaglets. Then as they grow, she helps with the hunting, too.

After 10 or 12 weeks, the eaglets can fly well, hunt and protect themselves. They are ready to leave the nest.

△ △ △

People and eagles get along quite well. But they haven't always. At one time, there were many more eagles than there are today. Then people began to shoot them for sport and for bounties (reward money paid for killing the eagles). People also killed eagles to protect farm animals, even though eagles ate very few. It was years before these birds were protected by law in North America.

Now some of the wild places where eagles live need protecting. Eagles need places with tall, old trees or cliffs. They need food and water that is free from chemical spray. If people can provide that, they will be "soaring with the eagles."

S·A·L·M·O·N

Hurdle Leapers

Masses of shiny salmon surge upstream. Powerful swimmers buck the current, stopping at nothing: a boulder, a waterfall, even a small dam. They bound, they spin, they leap—some more than six metres into the air. Even the word "salmon" comes from a Latin word meaning "to leap."

No wonder this amazing fish, which spends part of its life in fresh water and part in salt water, is so exciting. People love watching salmon swim up streams to lay eggs. They love fishing for salmon at sea and eating the catch at home. And they love telling stories—even stories of magic—about this incredible leaping fish.

Salmon live naturally in northern countries of the world. But so many people enjoy them that other countries have introduced the fish. Now salmon live on all continents, except Antarctica.

How Salmon Came to Be

A prophet was walking by the sea, wondering where his people might get more food. Then he had an idea. "I'll make something that lives in the water," he said to himself. "If the people can find food there, they won't depend so much on wandering land animals, like caribou."

The prophet took a willow stick and prayed that it would change into a living thing. Then he threw the stick into the sea.

Soon, a salmon appeared. It was wet and cold. "I don't want to live in the water," it said.

The prophet gently wrapped seaweed around the salmon to keep it warm until it was used to the cold. "But you must stay in the water and help feed my people," he said, tossing the fish back.

The fish obeyed, and that's how salmon came to be. Their lateral lines are the marks left by the seaweed.

—a story from the Inuit of the Arctic

In Canada, Atlantic salmon live on the east coast, and five kinds of Pacific salmon live on the west coast—sockeye, coho, chum, pink (the smallest) and chinook (the largest).

Salmon are sleek, well-built fish. They move swiftly by waving their strong bodies and using their fins as rudders. Their lateral lines—lines running along both sides of the body—sense movements of other fish in the water.

Salmon are able to hide from their enemies, too. These fish blend with what is beneath them, so they can't be seen easily from above. And the scales on their bellies are specially shaped so that salmon cast very little shadow.

Taking Off

Salmon hatch from eggs buried in the gravel of streams. At first, they live beneath the stones, eating their own yolk sacs. When that food is gone, they leave the gravel to feed on tiny water insects.

Over the next few weeks, the salmon drift along, searching for feeding areas and small lairs—hiding places among stones. There are a great many of these in a river, but there are even more tiny salmon. Most cannot find feeding areas and lairs, so they die in a few months. But the rest keep growing and developing.

Some kinds of salmon head downstream to salt water soon after they hatch. Others may live three years in fresh water before swimming to the sea. Two fish from the same batch of eggs may live very different lives: one spending most of its life in a stream and remaining very small; the other spending most of its life in the ocean and growing very large.

The Salmon Come to North America

A man once travelled halfway around the world to a place that was rich with salmon. He brought his son along to find a wife—one who could bring the salmon back with her. That way, the man knew his people would not go hungry.

They came to a village chief who agreed to give his daughter in marriage. "But you must learn to prepare the fish," he said.

At the wedding feast, the village people taught the strangers about the different kinds of salmon: how to cook them, how to dry them and how to smoke them. The men were told: "After you eat, always return the bones to the water. That way the salmon will return the next year."

Then the man, his son and the new bride travelled home, and the salmon followed their canoe. When they arrived, the man gave each group of salmon a river to spawn in. And from that time on, his people had plenty to eat.

—*a story from the Kwakwaka'wakw (formerly called the Kwakiutl) of Canada*

At Sea and Heading Home

Once at sea, salmon don't have to compete for living space. They travel loosely together in "schools," eating small animals, like shrimp. As

---

The Salmon Children

Long ago, there was a sad king and queen—sad because they had no children.

"I'll go to see if the Wise One can help us," said the king.

The Wise One listened carefully to the king, then told him to go down to the fishing boats. "Have someone catch you a salmon. Tell your cook to roast it but to take care not to burn it," said the Wise One. "Your wife—and no one else—must eat the fish. Then you shall have a child."

The king got a salmon, and the cook roasted it. But the fish was slightly burned. The cook rubbed the burnt spot off with her hand, then without thinking, licked her finger.

Later that year, the queen gave birth to a child. So did the cook. And throughout their lives, these two salmon children looked so much alike, no one could ever tell them apart.

—a story from Ireland

---

the salmon grow bigger, they feed on larger prey—usually other fish.

Salmon gain a lot of weight at sea. When there is plenty of food, some Atlantic salmon can gain nearly a kilogram in a month. When chinooks are fully grown (up to seven years old), they usually weigh up to 10 kilograms, but a few can weigh as much as 45 kilograms.

Most salmon spend much of their adult lives at sea. But when it is time to reproduce, they return to the streams where they began—although scientists are not sure exactly how the salmon find their way. For many salmon, this means a journey of hundreds of kilometres through the sea, then hundreds more upstream. Some salmon in the Fraser River swim all the way across British Columbia—a distance of about 1300 kilometres.

The salmon's journey is exhausting. The sockeye, for example, swims about 35 kilometres every day during its last month in the ocean. Then it fights swift currents, jumps rapids and often leaps over waterfalls as it swims upstream.

River Nesting

Usually, male salmon are the first to reach the spawning sites—places where salmon deposit and fertilize eggs. Then the females arrive to make their nests, called "redds." Each female chooses a spot at the bottom of the stream. She digs a hollow in the gravel by turning on her side, bending her body and swishing her tail. As she brushes the water back and forth, she shifts stones—a few at a time. Now and then, she uses her back bottom fin to check the depth of the hollow.

A male salmon waits close by. If other males come near, he scares them off by flaring his fins, opening his mouth and chasing them away. The female salmon chases off other females that approach her redd.

After several hours, the redd is deep enough for the female salmon to lay her first, reddish eggs. The male fertilizes the eggs by squirting them with white milt. He moves close beside the female. Their bodies quiver as the eggs are laid and fertilized at the same time. Then the female buries the eggs with gravel.

During the next few days, the female makes and fills more redds. She lays thousands of eggs that hatch in weeks—or maybe months—depending on the temperature of the water.

Salmon usually guard their redds for a few days, but they are very weak from spawning and their hard journey. Pacific salmon spawn only once, then die. About one out of every ten Atlantic salmon live after spawning. Some of them return to the ocean, then head back upstream to spawn again.

△   △   △

The salmon has many enemies, like other fish, mink, otters, herons, seals, dolphins and killer whales—or orcas. But people who pollute streams where salmon live and spawn are the worst. The fish can't exist without clean, cool water that has plenty of oxygen.

Today, Canada is trying to increase the numbers of salmon by reducing pollution and building channels that help the fish travel upstream. People are trying to be a friend to this amazing leaping fish.

W·O·L·V·E·S

Team Players

A bushy tail. Perky ears. Long, furry legs and big feet. The wolf looks like a big dog, and it is. But this dog is wild—a resident of forests, mountains, plains and brushlands.

For centuries, people around the world have feared wolves. These strong dogs sometimes killed farm and ranch animals, and many people have feared for their own safety. Some of them believed wolves were evil and told stories of werewolves—humans who magically changed into wolves.

But a wolf is neither evil nor magical, and it usually stays away from people. Today, it lives in a few parts of the United States, Europe and Asia, and across most of Canada.

Werewolves in the Woods

Two men found a small house in a forest. There they saw two people sleeping and two wolf skins hanging on the wall. The men took the skins and flung them across their backs.

Suddenly, the wolf skins closed around the men. When they tried to speak, they sounded like wolves. The men dropped to the ground and walked like wolves. They had become werewolves.

For nine days, the two werewolves roamed the forest. They attacked every person they found. On the tenth day, a memory of being human stirred in the men. The wolf skins loosened and fell off.

At once, the men built a fire and burned the skins so they would never become werewolves again.

—*a story from Scandinavia*

Canada's wolves are the timber or grey wolves—the largest of all wild dogs. They are usually grey or black. Some, like those in the Arctic, are white. Still, no two wolves look exactly alike.

How Wolves Live Together

Wolves are very social animals—like people. They usually live together in a pack of six or seven wolves, but some packs are much larger. Most packs are families: the parent wolves, their young and sometimes other closely-related wolves. The parents, which stay together for life, normally lead the pack.

Hunting for Food

A lone wolf can catch small animals, like mice and frogs. But wolves usually hunt in packs to catch big game, like deer, caribou, moose and elk.

When members of a pack hunt, they work together as a team. They may circle their prey or herd it into an enclosed place. They may take turns running hard until they tire their prey. Or they may split into teams: one to chase the prey towards the other team—or one to distract a herd while the other team grabs an animal.

Whichever way wolves catch their prey, they share the food among all members of the pack.

Caring for Pups

The male leader and other wolves in the pack help the female leader find a den—a safe place to give birth. It may be a cave or a hole, which the wolves dig. When the pups are born, they need the warmth and milk from their mother's body. So the pack hunts food for the mother wolf and delivers it right to the den.

When pups start to eat, the pack gets food for them, too. Wolves eat the meat, then bring it up from their stomachs. The warm, partly-digested food is just right for the pups.

Sometimes, a pack member looks after the pups so the mother wolf can join the other wolves on a hunt.

Having Fun

Wolf pups play a lot. On their own, they leap after butterflies and pounce on flowers. But wolf pups like to play with playmates best. They chase other pups and jump on them. They pretend to fight, nipping at ears and rolling over each other.

The pups also like to play with bigger, older wolves. Most of these wolves play gently and patiently with the pups.

The Wolf That Saved the Twins

Two brothers, called Amulius and Numitor, argued over which of them should be king. Finally, Amulius forced Numitor away and made himself king.

Years later, he discovered that Numitor's daughter had given birth to twin sons, Romulus and Remus. Amulius feared the twins would threaten his power one day, so he told his servants to drown them in the river. But the servants were afraid of the flooding river. They left the twins in a cradle on the bank and it floated away.

Downstream, the cradle washed ashore.

The babies were still alive, but they felt cold and hungry. Luckily, a female wolf heard their crying. She lifted them gently from their cradle and warmed them with her body. She let them drink her milk and licked them lovingly.

Eventually, the twins were raised by a herdsman and they returned to help Numitor become king. They also started a new city, called Rome, at the place where the wolf saved them.

—*a story from Italy*

Protecting Each Other

Besides people—and wolves from other packs—a grown wolf has no real enemies. Still, the male pack leader often watches from a lookout where he can spot any danger. And all pack members check the skies for eagles or hawks that can snatch away a wolf pup.

How Wolves "Talk"

Wolves use sounds and body movements to "talk" to each other. Scientists are just beginning to understand this talk, but they know it's used for many reasons, like helping wolves find each other and raising their pups.

Howling and Other Sounds

Many people use the word "spooky" to describe wolves howling. But most of the time, it's a happy sound—to the wolves. When they gather before a hunt, wolves howl to show they are excited and ready to go. After a hunt, they may howl their success to the young wolves—who howl back. And when a pup is born, wolves howl near the den.

The pack leader often starts the howling. Then each wolf joins in with its own note. Together, they build a whole chorus of sound.

Wolves also howl for more serious reasons, like finding each other after a hunt. When it's time to leave the pack and find a mate, a wolf howls to inform the pack and attract a wolf of the other sex.

Wolves howl to help keep other packs out of their hunting areas. They seem to say: "We're here, so stay away." Wolves can hear howling more than six kilometres away.

Besides howling, wolves growl—especially at pack members who misbehave—and they often whimper to their pups. A mother wolf, for instance, may whimper to call her pups out of the den.

Body Language

You smile when you're happy and shrug your shoulders to say: "I don't know." That's body language. A wolf uses it, too. Here are a few things that scientists think wolves say with their bodies:

- *Wow, I'm happy!*
  Tail wags. Eyes shine. Mouth hangs half-open. Body wiggles.
- *I love you.*
  Tongue licks another's face. Tail wags. Parent wolves rub their bodies and heads together.
- *Would you like to play?*
  The wolf leaps in front of another, front legs out flat. Tail wags fast.
- *Let's eat!*
  Pups nibble and lick an adult's mouth.

The Chief and the Leader of the Wolves

One long, stormy winter, when it was very hard to hunt or fish, the people had little to eat. Then they heard wolves howling in the woods and felt afraid.

But their chief listened closely and heard the wolves howl his name. One howl asked for help, so the chief bravely took his nephews and entered the dark woods.

A wolf pack circled the men, but the leader lay weakly in the snow, a bone stuck in its throat. The chief pulled the bone out, and the wolf licked his hand.

After that, the pack killed deer and other animals for the chief and his people all winter long.

—*a story from the Tsimshian of Canada*

- *Behave yourself.*
  Eyes stare for a long time (wolves normally avoid eye contact). Body crouches, ready to spring. Snout wrinkles. Mouth bares teeth. Teeth bite the loose skin at the back of a wolf's neck.
- *I'm more important than you are.*
  Tail rides high. Ears stand up. Fur fluffs out, back arches and legs straighten, all making the wolf look bigger.
- *You're more important than I am.*
  Tail hangs low. Ears lie back. Fur lies flat. When approaching a leader, a wolf keeps its body low and gently licks or nips the leader's snout.
- *Let's not fight.*
  Tail tucks in between the legs. Body flops on its back. Head lies back.

△   △   △

The world has few wolves compared to the number it once had. In several countries, they have completely disappeared. People trapped, shot and poisoned many. And as people created farms, ranches and cities, they left fewer places for wolves to live.

We are lucky that wolves still live across Canada. Now we must ensure their survival—not only for Canadians, but for the rest of the world.

The Wolf That Would Be Free

A starving wolf met a fat dog one night. "How do you get so much to eat?" asked the wolf.

"My owner feeds me for guarding the house," said the dog.

"I would like to work for my meals, too," said the wolf. So the dog started to take the wolf home. Then the wolf noticed a collar around the dog's neck and asked what it was for.

"Oh, that's what my chain fastens to," said the dog.

The wolf stopped suddenly and yelled: "Your chain? You mean your owner ties you up?"

"Sometimes," said the dog, "but I get all the food I can eat."

The wolf returned to the woods at once, saying: "I would rather starve than be someone's slave."

—*a story from Greece (one of Aesop's fables)*

R·A·V·E·N·S

Fun Seekers

A big, black bird with a purplish shine and a beak longer than your longest finger. That's the raven. It's a bold, noisy bird that looks a lot like a crow. But the raven is much larger.

Surprisingly, ravens can live almost everywhere—on sea coasts and mountain tops, on ice floes and deserts, in forests and some cities. Few other birds are able to live in so many different kinds of places.

Spread across much of Canada and the world, ravens are the subject of many stories. Some of them feature a very wise or brave raven; others, a tricky or magical bird. Some call the raven evil; others call it good. But whatever the raven is like in stories, in real life, it is a lively, playful bird.

Ravens Playing

Many scientists agree: ravens like to play. Their play may be part of the way they get attention or attract a mate. But playing—just having fun—seems to be a big part of being a raven.

What are some of the things they like to do?

- Pull each other's tail.
- Pass pebbles, beak to beak.
- Pretend to pass a stick, then yank it back.
- Toboggan down a snowbank on their backs, head first.
- Hang by their beaks, or hang upside down by one or two feet.
- Dart in and out of water spouts and sprays.
- Soar high in the sky, then dive down again.
- Turn hundreds of somersaults in the air.
- Pester a wolf by pecking its tail or diving at its head.

Ravens Feeding

Ravens are not fussy. They eat almost anything: dead animals, live animals, eggs—and some fruit, grain and seeds. Although they sometimes hunt and kill for food, ravens prefer to get their meals the easy way—from other animals. The raven is mainly a scavenger.

Hunting Food

Sometimes, ravens hunt animals as big or bigger than themselves. A pair of ravens may attack another bird by flying in relays, forcing it down, then pecking it on the head. With their strong beaks, they may even kill rabbits and young deer.

Along the seashore, ravens also eat shellfish. They pick up oysters and clams, then break into them by dropping them onto rocks.

Eating Leftovers

A lot of raven food is scraps and leftovers. Near cities and camps, ravens pick through garbage dumps for food. In the wild, they hang around after other animals have made a kill, waiting to snap up scraps.

To be around when scraps become available, ravens often follow hunters, like wolves, coyotes and bears. Or sometimes, ravens follow animals being hunted, like caribou. They may trail caribou herds for 50 kilometres in a day, just hoping a wolf pack will make a kill.

If ravens aren't around during a wolf attack, they can still arrive in time to eat leftovers. They just follow the sounds of the wolves, howling after a successful hunt.

Stealing Meals

Ravens don't always wait for scraps to eat. When they can, they steal food from other animals. Ravens chase birds, like crows, gulls and other ravens, that have something in their mouths. When the bird drops its food, the raven dives for it, catching the food in the air or scooping it off the ground. Ravens also pull birds, like doves, off their nests to steal eggs.

Why Ravens Are Black

Once, in an ice house, a raven was arguing with a large owl. They screeched and they squawked. And their screeches and squawks grew louder and louder.

Finally, the owl became so mad that it threatened to harm the raven. With its powerful feet, the owl grabbed a smoky lamp and turned it upside down over the raven.

Soot poured out. It covered the raven's whole head and body. The raven flew off, crying: "Kaq, kaq, kaq."

And that is why ravens are as black as soot today.

—*a story from the Inuit of the Arctic*

Ravens even steal from animals much bigger than themselves. They will swoop down on a grizzly bear that has caught a fish and hauled it out of the water. They will charge a young wolf so another raven can steal what the wolf was eating. Ravens have also been known to dig through a metre of snow to uncover food that mountain climbers have buried for later use.

Ravens Nesting

Lifelong mates, a pair of ravens work together to build a new nest or enlarge an old one—often in a tree or high on a cliff. Ravens make nests of sticks, mud and moss. They line them with grass or hair. Nests made bigger each year sometimes reach almost two metres in height.

The Raven Saves the Worker

A worker was digging near a large, heavy rock. The rock was about to fall, but the worker didn't notice.

A raven, flying by, dropped a pebble on the worker's head.

He shouted angrily at the raven but kept on digging.

Again, the raven dropped a pebble on the worker.

"Go away, you horrid bird," he yelled, shaking his fist.

Next, the raven flew to the beach. The raven grabbed a small board from a rotting boat and dropped it in front of the worker.

This time, the worker threw aside his shovel and picked up the wood. "Let's see if there's more where this came from," he said. He followed the raven to the beach to look for firewood.

Just after they left, the big rock came thundering down—right where the worker had been digging.

—a story from the United Kingdom

A female raven lays four to six greenish-blue eggs with brown or black blotches. After 20 days or so, the nestlings crack out of the eggs. Wearing patches of brown down, they don't look much like ravens at all.

Both parents work hard to feed the nestlings. Sometimes, ravens have to fly long ways for food, so they use the throat pouches in their necks to carry it home.

When the nestlings see their parents coming, they beg for food. They flutter their wings and stretch their mouths wide open. A parent bird sticks its beak right into these mouths to feed the nestlings.

After more than six weeks, the young ravens leave the nest. They flock together to search for food during their first year. Then they look for mates, build nests and start to raise their own young.

△   △   △

Today, ravens don't live in as many places as they once did. When herds of buffalo started to disappear on the Canadian prairies, so did the wolves that hunted them and the ravens that ate the leftovers. And some people killed many ravens for sport, or to protect chickens and sheep.

But ravens have been appearing in towns, like Whitehorse, Yukon Territory, where they are very welcome. In fact, in 1985, Yukon made the raven its official bird—a happy story about this fun-seeking animal.

Alone in the Nest

Mother raven laid five eggs in her nest, then stayed to keep them safe and warm. She sat on the eggs for many days while father raven brought her food to eat.

But when the eggs cracked open, both the ravens were amazed. "These little birds can't be ours," they thought. "They don't even look like ravens." So they left the little birds all alone.

The young birds were very hungry. They called out for food, but their parents brought them nothing. The little ravens fed only on tiny drops of dew that formed on the nest.

Then, black feathers began to grow on the young birds. Gradually, they began to look like ravens. The parent birds recognized them as their own and started to feed the hungry birds—just in time.

—*a story from Europe*

S·E·A·L·S

Depth Divers

Seals dart swiftly—gracefully—through the sea. Then they clamber onto shore and bask in the sun. As animals of both sea and land, seals are very unusual. They have fascinated people for centuries and appeared as characters in many stories. Some tales even feature seals that spend parts of their lives living on land—as people.

Several different animals in the world are called "seals":

- walruses;
- 14 kinds of eared seals—sea lions and fur seals; and
- 19 kinds of earless or "true" seals.

A better word to call all these animals is "pinnipeds." It means "fin-footed"—referring to the big, flat flippers they all have. They all have ears, too. Earless seals and walruses have only small openings on the sides of their heads, but they do have ears inside.

Of all pinnipeds, the walrus is the easiest to pick out. It is famous for its two tusks—metre-long teeth that help chip holes in ice and threaten other walruses. Sea lions are the pinnipeds often seen in zoos, especially the noisy, barking California sea lions. They are naturally playful—chasing bubbles, tossing seaweed and pretending to fight each other. Fur seals—the other kind of eared seals—are known for their thick fur coats and pointed noses. Earless or true seals, like all pinnipeds, are excellent divers and swimmers. They range widely in size—from 60 kilograms to four tonnes.

How Seals Came to Be

At one time, there were no seals. In fact, there were no animals in the sea. But a beautiful girl, called Sedna, lived with her father on the seashore.

A handsome hunter appeared in a kayak one day and said, "Come with me, Sedna, and you shall have everything you want."

Sedna went, but out at sea, she discovered the hunter was really a spirit bird, pretending to be a man. He flew her to an island where she felt sad and lonely.

Next year, Sedna's father tried to take her home in his kayak. The unhappy spirit bird chased after them, then dove into the sea. The gods were so angry with Sedna that they caused a fierce storm. Waves lashed the kayak.

To save himself, Sedna's father threw his daughter overboard. She grabbed onto the kayak, but her father struck her fingers again and again. As they broke, the fingers turned into seals and other sea animals.

Sedna sank to the bottom of the sea. There she became a powerful spirit, controlling all the animals she created.

—*a story from the Inuit of the Arctic*

Canada's Pinnipeds

In Canada, walruses live in the eastern Arctic. California and Steller's sea lions and northern fur seals live in the Pacific. And true seals live on all three of the country's coasts. Some harbor seals—one kind of true seal—swim up rivers and spend the rest of their lives in lakes.

Except for the harbor seals, Canada's true seals are named for their looks:

- Ribbon seals have white bands around their necks, shoulders and back ends.
- Bearded seals have thick sets of long, white whiskers.
- Ringed seals have rings around their spots.
- Harp seals have harp-like, horseshoe-shaped markings on their sides and back.
- Grey seals are usually plain grey in color.
- Male hooded seals have large hoods of skin on their heads.
- Male elephant seals have noses like short elephant trunks. They are also huge—like elephants. Weighing up to two tonnes, male elephant seals are Canada's biggest pinniped.

The Seal Returns to the Sea

A man was walking along the seashore when he heard singing coming from a cave. Outside the cave lay many seal skins. The man took one home and locked it in a closet.

Later that day, he saw a young woman crying by the cave. He was kind to her, and they came to love each other. But the woman often stared sadly out to sea.

Time passed. The man and woman married and had seven fine children. Then one day, the man went fishing and forgot to take the closet key. His wife found the seal skin. Sadly, she stared out to sea. Then she slipped on the skin and dove into the water.

After that, whenever the man fished, or his children walked along the shore, a seal swam nearby. And the man always caught many tasty fish; his children always found many pretty shells.

—*a story from Iceland*

Moving Around

On Land

Pinnipeds have flippers for limbs, which is something like having feet but no legs. That makes it hard for them to raise their sturdy bodies off the ground and move. Most true seals depend mainly on their body muscles to get them around—earthworm style. But the spine of the elephant seal helps it move in a special way: by arching its back, the seal raises its body so it can move along quite quickly on its front flippers. Eared seals and walruses use their slightly longer, stronger flippers to raise their bodies and waddle.

In Water

Pinnipeds may be clumsy on land, but they are graceful in water. That's a good thing because they spend much of their time at sea. Pinnipeds usually come ashore to soak up some sunshine, catch some sleep and—once a year—raise pups.

The pinniped is designed to swim. Harbor seal pups can even swim at birth. The pinniped's smooth head and body are shaped to slip easily through the water. Powerful back flippers propel true seals and walruses forward. Eared seals rely more on their front flippers, using them like oars to move swiftly through the water. Many pinnipeds swim long distances between their breeding and fishing spots.

Most pinnipeds can swoop, spin and dive through the water with ease. But the champion is the elephant seal. It swims far out to sea and hunts in the deepest water. Recently, researchers were amazed at an elephant seal that dove more than 1200 metres into the ocean. By comparison, a person who is scuba diving rarely goes deeper than 30 metres.

Growing Fat

Pinnipeds eat mainly fish and shellfish. They need plenty of food to keep them going—and to build up layers of body fat. That fat helps them float and keep warm in cold waters.

Fat also stores energy, which pinnipeds use as they need it. Many kinds of males are so busy at breeding times that they don't stop to feed. Some don't eat for three months, so they need their fat layers for energy.

Many kinds of female true seals go without food when they're caring for their young. These mothers use their stored fat to keep themselves alive. The fat also helps them produce enough milk for their pups. The milk is rich with fat and proteins, so the pups grow fast and build their own layers of fat.

The Smart Seal Gets the Salmon

A man on a boat was catching salmon when a big seal appeared at the end of his net. It started to eat some of the fish, so the man shot the seal. It fell backwards.

"That's the last I'll see of you," he muttered.

The next day, the man returned to his boat, but he didn't take his gun along. Imagine his surprise when he saw the same big seal waiting at the end of his net. One of its flippers was bandaged from the gunshot, but the seal was as lively as ever.

"He must be very smart to know I don't have my gun today," thought the man. And he wished the seal a long, long life.

—*a story from Ireland*

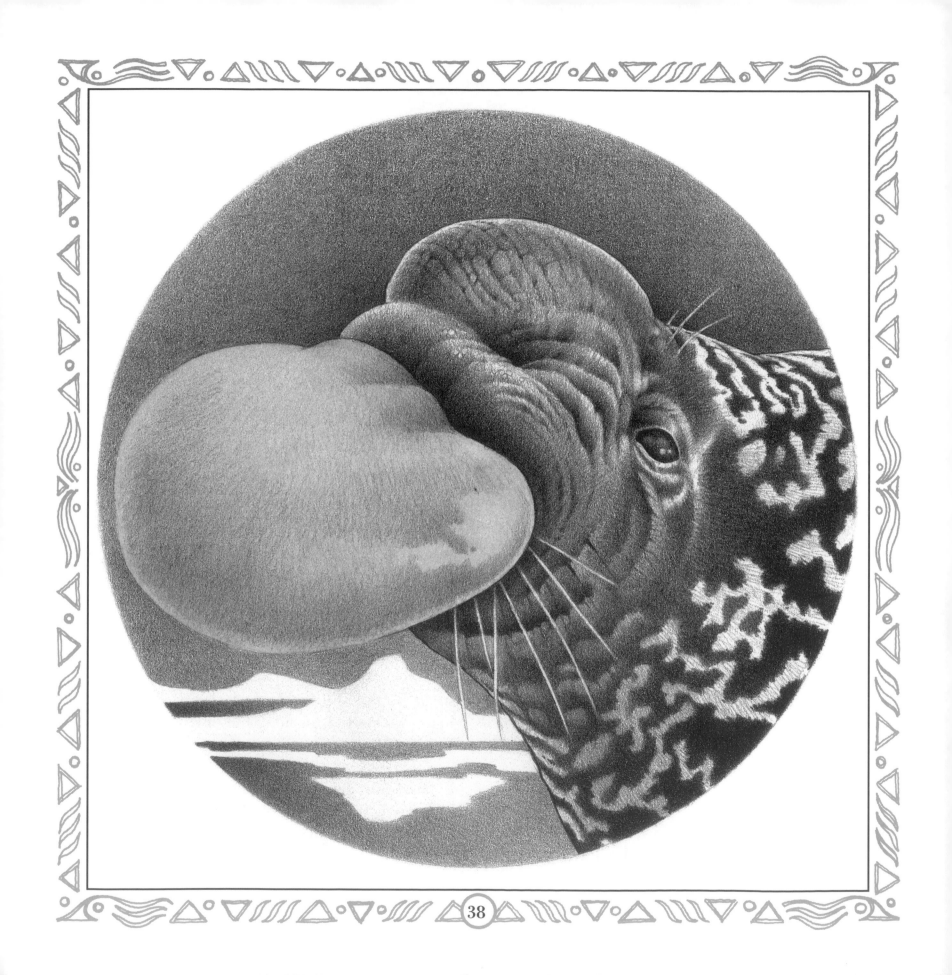

Blowing Noses

The nose of a grown male elephant seal is so long that the tip hangs about 30 centimetres below the seal's mouth. Often the nose just dangles. But sometimes, the seal fills it with air—especially during breeding seasons. The nose looks like a cushion that curves down and into the mouth.

The elephant seal snorts and bellows through his long nose. Then the sound bounces around in his open mouth and grows louder. The noise can travel more than a kilometre, scaring away other male elephant seals.

Male hooded seals have big, wrinkly noses that usually hang loosely in front of their mouths. When the seal blows his nose full of air, it forms a high cushion, twice the size of a football.

The hooded seal also blows against the skin that separates his nostrils, forming a red "balloon" about 15 centimetres across. As the balloon grows, it sticks out through one of the seal's nostrils.

Hooded seals usually blow their noses during breeding times or when they feel threatened. But sometimes, they blow them when they are just lying around. Scientists think that hooded seals simply enjoy "playing" with their noses.

Although killer whales—or orcas—and polar bears often hunt pinnipeds, human beings have been their worst enemies. People have hunted these animals for their oil and beautiful skins. People also have killed pinnipeds to protect fish catches.

Today, Canadians are killing fewer pinnipeds than they once did. And many people are working to protect the beaches where pinnipeds breed and the waters where they swim.

B·A·T·S

Night Fliers

Bats! Say the word and visions fill people's heads. Visions of creatures flying blindly through the night. Visions of wings and claws tangling in people's hair. Visions of fangs draining blood from human victims.

But let's set the record straight. Bats are not blind, and they never tangle themselves in hair. And the only blood-feeding bats, called "vampire bats," live in Central and South America. They bite sleeping animals, like cattle, and lap up some of their blood.

The truth is that most bats are harmless and very gentle. They're even easy for experts to tame and train. One scientist catches bats and teaches them to come when called—in just a few hours.

There are lots of bats on Earth. They live most everywhere, except the Arctic and Antarctic. And there are about 1000 kinds, in many sizes and colours. Some are strange looking, but others are as cute as dogs.

The Brave Woman and the Bat

At one time, a huge monster bat lived in the mountains near a village. Each night, the bat would swoop down and snatch anyone it found outside. The villagers had tried—without luck—to find its home and kill the bat.

Then a brave woman decided to help the villagers. One night, she hid a smouldering stick beneath her shawl and stood outside. Sure enough, the bat grabbed her and flew towards home.

As she went, the woman uncovered her stick, and it burst into flames. The villagers watched the fire streak across the sky and took off for the bat's home at once.

Before they could get there, the home caught fire and the monster bat died. After that, the villagers felt safe at night. But, to this day, no one knows what happened to the brave woman.

—*a story from South America*

42

Most of Canada has bats—21 kinds altogether. There are plain ones, like the little brown bat and the big brown bat. There are also handsome ones, like the hoary bat with its white-tipped fur and orange "collar," and the red bat with its long, soft fur and white markings.

How Bats Get Around

Bats are special. They are the only mammals on Earth that fly. (Mammals are warm-blooded animals—usually furry or hairy—that produce milk for their young.) Like you, bats have arms and hands with fingers and thumbs. But a bat's hand and finger bones are so long they form the framework of its wings.

Because the bat can move each finger and thumb separately, the bat is an amazing flier. It can hover, make sharp turns, twist this way and that, dive and swoop. It can flip up in the air and come to rest upside down—the normal position for a bat. The fact that its knees bend backwards helps the bat land this way.

Using Echoes

Bats that hunt insects make high squeaks that help them target their prey. These squeaks also help bats avoid bumping into things in the dark. When the sounds hit something, they bounce back—as echoes—to the bat's big ears. These echoes form a picture in the bat's brain, telling it about the size, shape and feel of whatever the sounds bounce off. The echoes also tell the bat how far away something is, especially if it is closer than three metres This way of using sounds and echoes is called "echolocation."

Using Eyes

To sense things that are farther away, these bats also use their sight. Although their eyes are very small, the bats see at least as well as other small animals. The bats use eyesight to watch for enemies and to find their way to and from winter homes.

Why Bats are Night Creatures

When the world began, the king called a meeting of all things. He sent a dove to fetch the moon and a bat to fetch the sun. The dove went at once, bringing the moon quickly. But the bat took its time, and the sun arrived late.

The king was very angry with the sun, so he gave the easiest jobs to the moon and the hardest ones to the sun. That made the sun very angry with the bat.

One day, the bat asked the sun, "Would you please help my mother? She's sick."

"Okay," said the sun, "Come to me tomorrow before I start my daily trip across the sky."

But the bat took its time and arrived late. And the angry sun refused to go back to help the bat's mother.

From that day on, the bat avoided the sun, going outside only at night.

—a story from Africa

When the cold weather starts, bats take off. Some don't go far. They just fly to a cave or an old, sheltered mine to "hibernate"—sleep deeply through the winter. Others may fly several hundred kilometres to another region for the winter. Scientists think bats may watch for landmarks, like mountains and lakes, to help them find their way.

In spring, the bats return—usually to the same place. People have seen the hoary bat, for instance, fly back to the same branch in the same tree.

What Bats Do at Night

All night, while you're asleep, bats are out and about. Most of the time, they are busy hunting food. The darkness doesn't slow them down. In fact, bats seem less busy when there's lots of moonlight—maybe because their enemies can spot them more easily.

In Canada, bats are the main enemies of night-flying insects. Some bats eat lots of mosquitoes. The expert, the little brown bat, catches about 600 mosquitoes in an hour. Some bats feed mainly on beetles; others prefer moths. But they all eat insects that are pests to gardeners and farmers.

Using their squeaks and echoes to find insects, bats swoop after them, mouths open and ready to chomp. Bats also use their wings and the skin between their back legs to scoop insects towards their mouths.

Most bats also drink water at night. They fly very low across lakes or rivers—good places to catch insects, too—and dip their mouths into the surface.

How Bats Care for Pups

Female bats give birth in late spring. Most have just one pup a year, but some kinds have more.

A newborn bat pup is tiny and helpless. It depends on its mother to nurse it—usually for three to four weeks. Meanwhile, it learns to do what bats do: fly, hunt food and avoid enemies, like owls, snakes, weasels and fish.

Before they give birth, some kinds of female bats gather in large groups. Their pups like the heat bats create when they amass in these nurseries. Little brown bats form nurseries of 300 to 800 bats. Big brown bats prefer slightly "cooler" nurseries—fewer than 300.

Right from birth, a pup can hang upside down on its own. But during the day, it may use one wing to cling to its mother. Its teeth cling to her nipple. At night, the mother leaves her young pup hanging with the other pups in the nursery and hunts insects for herself.

When she returns, the mother bat tries to remember where she left her pup. She also sniffs and listens for it. Each of the pups makes its own special smell and sound. The mother bat keeps nursing her pup until it can fly well and hunt food on its own.

With all the good that bats do—eating mosquitoes and insects that harm farm and garden plants—it's surprising so many people dislike them. Yet every year, people deliberately kill bats. They also accidentally kill bats by spraying chemicals to get rid of insects and by disturbing places where bats live. But as more people realize how helpful and harmless bats really are, they may try to protect these very special animals.

The Bat and the Weasels

A weasel caught a little bat that had fallen to the ground.

"Please let me go," the bat begged.

"I can't. I'm an enemy of birds," said the weasel.

"Look at me," yelled the bat. "I'm not a bird. I'm a mouse."

The weasel looked again, and it let the bat go.

Later, another weasel caught the same bat.

"Please let me go," the bat begged.

"I can't. I'm an enemy of mice," said the second weasel.

"Look at me," yelled the bat. "I'm not a mouse, I'm a bird."

The weasel looked again, and it let the bat go.

—a story from Greece (one of Aesop's fables)

B·E·A·V·E·R·S

Bark Munchers

Check your pocket for a beaver. There's one on a Canadian nickel. That's because the beaver is so important to Canada. A few hundred years ago, beaver trapping led people across much of the land that later became Canada. The beaver was adopted as the country's national animal and played a part in many stories.

People trapped beavers mainly for their beautiful, thick fur. It grows in two layers: a soft, woolly undercoat and long, silky outer hair. The fur—which may be blond, reddish, brown or black—is almost waterproof.

Beavers feed on plants—mainly tree bark—but in the spring, they eat a lot of water plants. Sometimes, they eat other things, like berries, wild roses and—if they're near gardens—carrots, corn and potatoes.

Beaver Lives Another Day

For many years, people knew the beaver as a gentle animal with a fine fur coat. Yet some hunters killed the beaver for glands that were supposed to contain medicine.

One day, hunters were tracking a beaver through the woods. "They are after my glands," thought the beaver. "If I rip them out and leave them for the hunters, my life will be spared." So the beaver did just that.

The hunters, getting what they wanted, left the beaver alone. After that, whenever hunters chased the beaver, it would rise up on its back legs. It would show that its glands were gone—and it would live another day.

—*a story from Europe*

Unlike most animals, beavers never stop growing. Each year, they get bigger and bigger until they die, usually at about age 10. They are the largest rodents in North America, weighing up to 35 kilograms.

Worldwide, beavers also live in Europe and Asia. In Canada, they live right across the country—in ponds, lakes and rivers in forested areas.

Beavers as Swimmers

With its short legs, the beaver walks slowly. But in water, it zips along at eight kilometres an hour. The beaver swims with its webbed back feet and steers with its wide, flat tail. It seems so at home in the water that early scientists thought the beaver was a fish—especially because its tail is covered with fish-like scales.

When the beaver dives, a set of clear eyelids covers its eyes, improving its sight. The beaver's ears and nostrils close. And flaps of skin behind its front teeth keep water out of its mouth. The beaver can hold its breath for about 15 minutes.

To waterproof its fur, the beaver takes oil from a gland in its own body. It uses a split claw on one of its back feet to comb the oil through the fur. The combing also removes tangles that could slow swimming.

The beaver swims all year round. During winter, its body fat and thick fur help keep it warm in the water. In the spring, young beavers learn to swim, starting when they are just five days old. Usually, they learn in a few hours.

Beavers are safer in water than on land. But they always watch out for enemies, especially otters, which can outswim beavers. At any sign of danger, the beaver whacks its tail on the water to warn others.

Beavers as Loggers

Beavers cut down trees to get bark for food, and twigs and branches for building houses and dams. Using strong jaw muscles and sharp front teeth, beavers gnaw through small trees in minutes. A "logging" beaver stands on its back legs—propped up by its flat tail—and chews around a trunk until the tree falls down.

A hard, orange coating protects the beaver's front teeth from breaking. They are always sharp and always growing, so the beaver must gnaw wood to keep them trimmed.

A beaver takes the trees that are closest to the water and gnaws them into logs. It may roll or push the logs with its front paws, or its head and nose. Although the beaver is small, it is very strong.

When the closest trees are gone, the beaver heads to the woods for more. It may clear paths to push logs back to the water. Sometimes, the beaver digs a canal between the water and the woods so it can float logs back. Beaver canals can be up to 100 metres long.

Beavers as Builders

Beavers build dams and houses, called "lodges," in forest ponds and slow-moving rivers. They stick small branches and twigs into the dirt beneath the water, holding it all down with rocks. Then they build upwards, using roots, twigs and

Beavers and People Make Good Friends

A man was watching beavers cut down trees near a stream. He was amazed at the way they could chew through wood. "I wish they could log for us," he said to his wife.

"We'd be glad to," said a beaver, startling the couple.

Then the beaver signalled to other beavers. Together, they cut down lots of trees—some to build a house and some to build a dam.

The man and woman lived happily in the house. And every year, they drew water from the stream behind the dam to help their turnips grow. They were so grateful that they planted more trees for the beavers to chew. And the couple always protected the beavers from hunters who wanted their beautiful fur.
—*a story from French Canada*

branches until the dam or lodge is above water. Sometimes beavers press down the material with rocks that are almost as heavy as themselves. With their front paws, they scoop up mud to fill in any small spaces.

Although a beaver dam and a lodge are built with the same materials, the dam stretches— like a wall—right across a pond or river. A beaver lodge is more like a dome with an open area inside. It is usually surrounded by water.

Beavers enter a lodge underwater and scramble up ramps to the dry space in the dome above. That's where a beaver family eats and rests. A lodge often holds eight to ten beavers: two parents, three to four young beavers and three to four babies, called "kits." For a larger family, a lodge may have two rooms.

During winter, the heat from the beavers' bodies warms the lodge. The mud in the cracks freezes hard, keeping heat in—and enemies out. Sometimes, beavers make so much heat that the snow on the roof of their lodge melts.

Even when water freezes over, beavers can swim beneath the ice. Their dams keep rivers and ponds deep year round so that beavers can swim to and from their lodges. And they can also reach their winter food—a pile of logs and branches that beavers usually store underwater.

Two beavers can build a small dam overnight, but they need several nights to build a large one. One of the biggest beaver dams in Canada stretched more than 1.5 kilometres across the Bow River in Saskatchewan.

But beavers can't dam fast-flowing rivers or lakes—so they don't build lodges there. Instead, beavers simply dig dens in the dirt banks.

△　△　△

In the past, people hunted many beavers, especially when beaver fur was popular. In Canada, too many beavers were trapped. But laws protecting them have brought their numbers back up. As a result, you will likely find beavers in Canada for many years—even outside your pocket.

Fantastic Beaver Tales

A traveller to North America had seen many things, but one of the most amazing was a beaver colony. When he returned to Europe, he told people about it.

"Beavers are wonderful builders," he said. "They build all the time. They even make their own houses."

The people were very interested, so the traveller told them more: "Beavers make houses that are three-storeys tall. They use their flat tails—like trowels—to plaster the houses with mud."

The people were amazed, which pleased the traveller even more. He continued: "The beaver colony is very organized. It has a government. It makes laws. It has officers who make beavers obey the laws. It..."

But the people began to shake their heads and walk away. The traveller had gone too far.

—*a story from North America*

O·W·L·S

Trick Players

Put oversized eyes in an oversized head. Add a hooked beak that looks like a nose. Place it all on top of a thick, fluffy body, and meet the owl—one of the world's most bewitching birds.

In several countries, people believed that owls were wise or magical. Many saw owls as signs of death. Some folks even believed that owls were the angry souls of dead people.

But an owl is simply a bird. It lives on every continent, except Antarctica. Worldwide, there are more than 130 kinds of owls; about 15 kinds live in the forests, meadows and prairies of Canada. Screech-owls even live in cities.

Owl Coats

Owls have magnificent, thick coats made of feathers—more feathers than most other birds. These coats keep owls snug in the wind, and dry in the rain; warm in the winter, and cool in the summer.

Owl Omen

One fall day, a man took his son to the woods to fix an old cabin. A visitor, named Felix, went along for the company. But soon the man and his son returned.

"Why are you home early, and where's Felix?" asked the man's wife.

"We saw the white owl and left the woods at once," said the man. "But Felix wouldn't come with us. He doesn't believe in the white owl's evil."

By nightfall, Felix still hadn't returned, so the next morning, the man and his son went to look for him. As they walked through the woods, they kept a careful watch for the white owl.

Not far from the cabin, they found Felix. He was pinned to the ground by a tree that had fallen across his chest. And from the distance came the cold, clear call of the white owl.

—a story from French Canada

When owlets hatch, they grow fluffy coats of down. Most owlets moult the down as they sprout feathers. But some, like the great grey owls, keep their down—like warm underwear—beneath their feathers. That helps them live through very cold weather.

A feathered coat also helps the owl hide from enemies, like bigger birds and foxes. The colours of the feathers blend with the owl's background so its enemies don't notice the bird. Many owls are grey or brown with dark spots and streaks, like tree trunks. The burrowing owl, a ground bird, is the colour of dry earth and grass, speckled to look like splashes of sunshine. The snowy owl is creamy white, like the snow.

Feathers even help some owls "talk." Long-eared and short-eared owls, great horned owls and screech-owls have tufts of feathers on the tops of their heads. These tufts look like ears, but they're not. The owl sticks them forward as if to say: "Stay away. This is my area." It lays them down and back as if to say: "Be kind to me."

But the most amazing thing about the owl's feathery coat is how it helps the night-hunting owl fly silently. A velvet-like coating on its wing feathers cushions the air that rushes by. And the feathers on the wings' front edges are fluffy and fringed. That also deadens sound.

Owl Prowls

Owls spend much of their time hunting for food. They eat lots of mice and little birds. Small owls also eat small things, like insects and frogs. Big owls also eat big things, like squirrels, rabbits and skunks.

All owls use their super-sharp claws to catch and kill animals. A large owl can kill a skunk with a single thrust to the head.

Owls see very well, day and night. But they can never move their eyes to see side to side. Instead, they must turn their whole heads. An owl's neck contains twice as many bones as your

Why Burrowing Owls Have Spots

Once, when burrowing owls were all black in colour, a grandfather owl was teaching some young owls to dance. They had to bob and bow with bowls on their heads, and the bowls were filled with foam.

A passing coyote laughed when it saw the owls. "I could dance better than you," it said. "Give me a bowl."

But when the coyote tried to dance, it staggered and stumbled. It flopped this way and that.

The young owls laughed so much they spilled the foam from their bowls. It splashed all over them, making grey-white splotches on their feathers. And nobody—not even the grandfather owl—was ever able to remove them.

—*a story from the Zuni of the United States*

neck does, so the owl can almost turn its head right around.

Many—but not all—owls hunt at night. Those that do, have special sight and hearing that make them excellent hunters. Owl eyes are huge and take in much more light than your eyes do. Some scientists say that owls can see at least 50 times more clearly at night than people can.

Why Some Owls Fly Only at Night

There once was a little wren who lost all its feathers. Each of the other birds decided to give one of its own feathers to the wren.

But not the owl. "I need all my feathers for the cold weather ahead," it said.

This made the king very angry. "From now on, you will be the most pitiful bird," he told the owl. "You will leave your home only at night. If you try to go out during the day, the other birds will chase you and punish you."

From that day on, some owls flew only at night.

—a story from France

Even if there is no light, a night-hunting owl can hunt well. It depends on its wonderful sense of hearing. Hidden beneath its head feathers, the owl has huge ears. For their size, they contain the largest ear drums of any bird. The owl can hear the footsteps of a mouse and swoop after it with deadly accuracy. That's why the wings of these owls move so silently. If they slapped the air like other birds' wings, the owl couldn't hear the soft sounds of its prey.

Owl Tricks

Owls are no magicians, but they know a few tricks. They play them on their enemies to avoid capture. Here are just a few:

- Owls make themselves look tough. They fluff up their feathers until they appear twice their real size. Then they spread out their large wings and sway from side to side.
- One of the smallest owls in Canada, the flammulated owl, throws its voice like a ventriloquist. Its hoot seems to come from one tree, while the owl is in another.
- The northern pygmy owl has eyes in the back of its head—or so it seems. Black-and-white markings, which look like big eyes, make enemies think the owl sees them, even from behind.
- To protect owlets in the nest, the long-eared owl hops about, pretending to have a broken wing. As it hops away from the nest, its enemy follows. Then, suddenly, the owl flies off.
- If an enemy comes close, snowy owlets pretend they are dead.
- In their underground nest, burrowing owlets imitate the sound of rattlesnakes. That scares away their enemies.

△　△　△

As tricky as the owl is, it has trouble outtricking its worst enemy—humans. People harm owls by removing forests and farming grasslands where some kinds of owls live. Even so, owls help people just by doing what owls do best: eating lots of the insects and mice that damage crops.

The Owl That Saved the Prince

Prince Genghis Khan was out with his small army one night. Suddenly, his enemies appeared and chased him. The prince had to hide under a bush.

While Genghis Khan's enemies searched for him, an owl flew by. It perched on the very bush where the prince was hiding. When the prince's enemies came near, they saw the owl and thought, "No bird would perch close to a person." So they moved on.

Genghis Khan and his army were very grateful to the bird for tricking their enemies. From that day on, they respected the owl and wore its feathers on their headgear, especially at festivals.

—*a story from Asia*

W·H·A·L·E·S

Cloud Spouters

Giants are the stuff of many stories, but some whales are giants in real life. The largest animal in the world is the blue whale. It stretches about 25 metres from end to end—about as long as two trailer-trucks parked one behind the other. And the blue whale weighs nearly as much as three loaded trailer-trucks—about 100 tonnes.

Although whales live their whole lives in water, they are mammals—not fish. That means they are warm-blooded animals that produce milk for their young.

A whale breathes air into its lungs—just as you and other mammals do. But instead of a nose, a whale uses a blowhole on top of its head. Some kinds of whales have two blowholes.

Why Whales Blow Clouds

A long time ago, when the Wise One wanted to cross the water, he climbed onto a whale's back and ordered the whale to swim.

As they approached shallow water near the shore, the whale became afraid. The Wise One urged the whale on, but it ran aground.

"I'm stuck," cried the whale. "I'm stuck on land forever."

"Don't worry, you shall always live at sea," said the Wise One. And he shoved the whale back into deep water and gave it a reward: his own pipe.

Relieved and happy, the whale swam away, smoking the Wise One's pipe. And that is why—even today—whales blow big, white clouds into the sky.

—*a story from the Passamaquoddy of the United States*

When a whale comes to the water's surface, it breathes out of its blowhole. It spouts a big cloud of vapor that looks like your breath on a cold day. Then the whale takes in some fresh air. Before it dives under the water again, it closes its blowhole.

The whale is a very strong swimmer. A sturdy tail with two big fins, called "flukes," moves up and down to power the whale through the water.

Whales live in all of Earth's oceans; a few are found in rivers and lakes. Of the 76 kinds of whales in the world—including dolphins and porpoises—at least 20 live in Canadian waters and about a dozen more visit Canada regularly.

Toothy and Toothless

There are two main groups of whales: those with teeth and those without. Toothed whales eat mostly fish and squid. They use their teeth to grab—not chew—their food, so they usually swallow their prey whole.

Some toothed whales dive deep into the ocean to find food; others feed near the surface. Scientists estimate that the sperm whale, the only giant toothed whale, dives as deep as 3000 metres. The much smaller killer whale—or orca—often hunts closer to the surface in family herds, called "pods." Besides fish and squid, some orcas also eat mammals, like seals, sea lions and other whales.

Toothless or "baleen" whales eat small fish and tiny animals, such as krill, which are like shrimp. The whales filter the food from the water by using their baleen—several hundred plates that hang from the upper jaw. On some whales, these plates are up to two metres long and about a centimetre apart. They feel something like fingernails, but the inside edge of each plate is bristly, like a broom.

Some baleen whales swim along with their mouths open, sucking up tonnes of water and all the animals floating in it. Then they force the water out through their baleen. Only the food remains for the whales to swallow.

These baleen whales need lots to eat because they are so big. The gigantic blue whale eats a few tonnes of food every day, scooping it up near the surface of the water.

The big grey whale, however, swims along the ocean bottom. It scoops up mouthfuls of sand and mud, then strains everything out except the food. It can also feed by pushing water out of its mouth to stir up the seafloor, then sucking in whatever it raises.

Another baleen whale, the humpback, sometimes swims around and around beneath a school of fish, making bubbles with its breath. The bubbles rise in a net-like circle around the fish. Then the humpback charges up through the circle, gulping the water and the fish. Its throat expands so it can take in lots.

Why Whales Stay at Sea and Elephants Stay in the Woods

A rabbit on the shore spotted a whale. "I could pull you out of the water onto the land," said the rabbit.

"That's impossible," laughed the whale.

"Meet me at noon. I'll show you," said the rabbit, walking on. Soon it met an elephant in the woods.

"I could pull you out of the woods into the sea," said the rabbit.

"That's impossible," laughed the elephant.

"Meet me at noon. I'll show you," said the rabbit.

At noon, the rabbit tied one end of a very long rope around the whale in the water and the other end around the elephant in the woods. Then the rabbit stood where neither animal could see it and yelled: "Pull!"

Without looking back, the whale pulled the elephant to the edge of the sea. Without looking back, the elephant pulled the whale to the sandy shore. Back and forth they went until the rope snapped.

Then the whale swam far out to sea where it stayed; the elephant went deep into the woods where it stayed. And they both thought, "How strong that rabbit is!"

—a story from the Bahamas

Sounds and Songs

Oceans are huge bodies of water. They're so huge that whales would have a hard time finding their way—and each other—if they couldn't use sounds.

All whales make sounds. But the toothed beluga makes so many different squeals, squeaks, whistles, barks and chirps that early whale hunters called it a sea-canary.

Like bats, toothed whales use echolocation: they make sounds, then listen for their echoes. The whale uses these echoes to discover how big something is, how far away it is and which way it is heading. Many toothed whales use clicks and whistles to reach others and bring a group together.

Baleen whales also make sounds, especially low ones, like moans, sighs or even burp-like noises. But the sounds of a male humpback whale range from low to high. They form patterns that make songs, lasting up to 30 minutes each. Often the humpback sings them over and over again for hours—maybe to attract a mate or to warn off another male. Scientists aren't sure, but they do know that humpback songs are the loudest animal songs on Earth.

These Amazing Whales

Whales are amazing animals. Some of them are huge and long-living. Some display strange features or behaviour. Here are just a few surprising facts about Canadian whales:

Amazing Records

- Biggest brain: the large square head of the sperm whale contains about nine kilograms of brain.
- Longest tooth: the male narwhal, called the unicorn whale, has a tusk-like tooth nearly three metres long. It grows straight out through the whale's lip.
- Longest life: fin whales live up to 100 years.

Amazing Behaviour

- Spyhopping: whales slowly "stand" straight up in the water so their eyes can peak out near the water's surface.

Whale Island

Once, a huge whale was basking in the warm sun; its long back lay above the surface of the sea. The whale had been sleeping for several hours when some sailors appeared in lifeboats from a storm-wrecked ship.

The sailors were thrilled when they spotted the whale's back. It looked like sand, so they thought they had reached an island. They staked their boats to the whale and built a large fire on "shore" to cook dinner.

The heat from the fire woke the whale. At once, it dove deep into the sea, taking the sailors and their lifeboats with it. And none, except the whale, were ever seen again.

—*a story from Europe*

Whale Meets the Buddha

Long ago, in the deepest water, lived the biggest whale of them all. It was so big that people many kilometres away could see it spout vapor high into the sky.

Then one day, a little fish told the mighty whale: "I have heard people talk of a bronze Buddha—a statue—bigger than anything on Earth. Its face, alone, is two-and-a-half metres long."

The whale was amazed, but angry. "Nothing is bigger than I," it told the fish.

Still, the whale decided to see this Buddha. It swam a long way, then walked across land to a big temple. The whale called to the Buddha inside.

A huge statue appeared in the doorway and asked kindly, "What do you want?"

"They say you are bigger than I," said the whale. "Can that be?"

The Buddha called a priest to measure them. After many hours, he said, "You two are exactly the same size."

"Ah," said the Buddha, smiling. "I may be the largest on land, but you, my friend, are the largest at sea."

And the whale went home, feeling contented.

—*a story from Japan*

- Lobtailing: whales lift their flukes up high, then slam them on the water. They may do this again and again for an hour or more.
- Breaching: whales leap partly—or completely—out of the water, making a thundering noise as they splash back down.
- Hitchhiking: small whales catch rides on waves caused by boats or big whales, like humpbacks or fin whales.
- Herding: some dolphins travel in herds of several thousand.
- Migrating: each year, grey whales travel 8000 to 11000 kilometres from cold Arctic waters to warm Mexican waters and back again. That is one of the longest annual trips of any mammal on Earth.
- Speed-diving: in just two minutes, the northern bottlenose whale can dive about 900 metres straight down.
- Breath-holding: the sperm whale can hold its breath for about two hours during deep dives.

△　　△　　△

Whales have only a few natural enemies, like orcas and sharks. But human hunters have killed many whales, seriously shrinking their numbers. In 1972, all commercial whale hunting in Canada was banned, but some kinds of whales are still rare today. Further, many small whales die when they accidentally get caught up in fishing gear. Let's hope the future has a place for these amazing animals—outside of storybooks.

List of Stories

Story Permissions

The stories in this book are original adaptations of old stories, many of which were once passed on from person to person—and in some cases, from country to country—before being written down. The author and the publisher, however, respect the expressed cultural right of Canadian Indians to tell and retell their own stories. Therefore, this book includes only those Indian stories for which permission to adapt was received:

- "Why Eagles See Well" adapted from "How the Eagle Got Sharp Eyes" in *Kwakiutl Legends* by Chief James Wallas and Pamela Whitaker. Vancouver: Hancock House Publishers Ltd., 1981 and 1989.
- "The Salmon Come to North America" adapted from "A Salmon Story" in *Kwakiutl Legends* by Chief James Wallas and Pamela Whitaker. Vancouver: Hancock House Publishers Ltd., 1981 and 1989.
- "The Chief and the Leader of the Wolves" adapted from "Gamlugyides and the Prince of the Wolves" in *The Princess and the Sea-Bear* by Joan Skogan. Vancouver: Polestar Press Ltd., 1992 (previously published by the Metlakatla Band Council, Prince Rupert, B.C.).

Permission to adapt these stories is gratefully acknowledged.

Index

About the Author

Diane Swanson lives on Vancouver Island, B.C. Her articles on nature and wildlife have appeared in children's magazines *Ranger Rick* and *Owl*. She has also written science and social studies texts for Canadian schools and is the author of *A Toothy Tongue and One Long Foot: Nature Activities for Kids*.

About the Illustrator

Douglas Penhale is a freelance artist living in Saltspring Island, B.C. An avid interest in nature, coupled with a move to the West Coast, turned him from commercial art to wildlife illustration. His nature drawings and cartoons have been featured in many books and magazines, and he was the Grand Prize Winner at the International Cartoon Festival in 1985.